P9-DOH-370

bake me I'm yours...

cupcake

love

Zoe Clark

David and Charles

www.rucraft.co.uk

A DAVID & CHARLES BOOK

Copyright © David & Charles Limited 2010

David & Charles is an F+W Media Inc. company
4700 East Galbraith Road, Cincinnati,
OH 45236

First published in the UK in 2010
Reprinted in 2011, 2012

Text and designs copyright © Zoe Clark 2010
Layout and photography copyright © David &
Charles 2010

Zoe Clark has asserted her right to be identified
as author of this work in accordance with the
Copyright, Designs and Patents Act, 1988.

All rights reserved. No part of this publication
may be reproduced, stored in a retrieval
system or transmitted, in any form or by
any means, electronic or mechanical, by
photocopying, recording or otherwise, without
prior permission in writing from the publisher.

The designs in this book are copyright and must
not be made for resale.

The author and publisher have made every
effort to ensure that all the instructions in the
book are accurate and safe, and therefore
cannot accept liability for any resulting injury,
damage or loss to persons or property,
however it may arise.

Names of manufacturers and products are
provided for the information of readers, with
no intention to infringe copyright or trademarks.

A catalogue record for this book is available
from the British Library.

ISBN-13: 978-0-7153-3781-3 hardback
ISBN-10: 0-7153-3781-5 hardback

Printed in China by RR Donnelley
for David & Charles
Brunel House   Newton Abbot   Devon

Acquisitions Editor Jennifer Fox-Proverbs
Assistant Editor Jeni Hennah
Project Editor Beth Dymond
Design Manager Sarah Clark
Art Editor Charly Bailey
Designer Victoria Marks
Photographer Sian Irvine
Production Controller Kelly Smith
Pre-Press Natasha Jorden

David and Charles publish high-quality books
on a wide range of subjects. For more great
book ideas visit: www.rucraft.co.uk

Contents

introduction...

Cupcakes have always been extremely popular, as they are so quick and easy to make. In the last few years, cupcakes have become incredibly fashionable, and we have seen so many little cupcake boutiques popping up and selling a variety of delicious flavours, usually decorated with decadent amounts of buttercream and finished with a scattering of brightly coloured sprinkles.

Cupcake Love takes this a little further and includes some very pretty and highly decorative designs that scream romance. Unlike the cupcakes you find on the high street, each project requires some basic sugarcrafting skills to create the decorations that make them unique. Naturally, because of the theme, a lot of the designs involve flower making in the form of roses and blossoms. I have also used a number of other techniques for which I have given step-by-step instructions to make each design easily achievable, even for beginners.

Cupcake making is fun and really rewarding. Not only can cupcakes be extremely delicious but they can also become a delightful little decorative work of art in themselves. I hope that all of the designs in the following pages will inspire you to have a go and experiment with making your own cupcakes to suit your personal taste and the occasion.

Good luck!

Zoë

X

www.zoeclarkcakes.com

basic tools and equipment

Before you begin to make and decorate your cupcakes, it's a good idea to be prepared. Included here is a list of basic tools and equipment that you will need to make and decorate any cupcake. More specific tools and equipment are listed for the individual designs in the 'you will need' section at the start of each project.

basic tool kit

1. **Electric mixer with paddle attachment:** to make cupcakes, buttercream and royal icing.
2. **Mixing bowls:** for mixing ingredients.
3. **Kitchen scales:** to accurately weigh your cupcake ingredients.
4. **Wire racks:** to cool the cakes.
5. **Spoons or disposable piping (pastry) bags:** to fill the cupcake cases.
6. **Spatula** or **large spoon:** to gently fold in your various ingredients.
7. **Small saucepan:** for heating ingredients on the hob (stove) – not pictured.
8. **Pastry brush:** for brushing ingredients such as sugar syrup or apricot masking jam on to your cupcakes.
9. **Scissors:** for making piping (pastry) bags and snipping off the ends.
10. **Cupcake tins (standard and mini):** for baking cupcakes.

decorating equipment

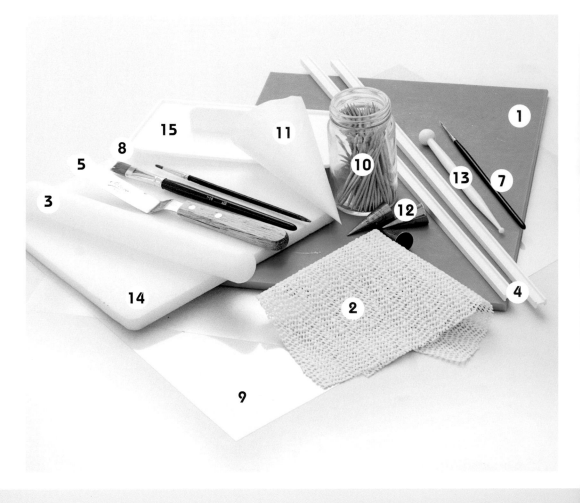

1. **Non-stick board:** for rolling out icing on.
2. **Non-slip mat:** to place underneath your board to prevent it from slipping.
3. **Small non-stick rolling pin:** for rolling out icing.
4. **Spacers:** to give a guide to the thickness of icing.
5. **Palette knives:** for applying buttercream and ganache to your cupcakes.
6. **Small sharp knife:** for cutting and shaping icing – not pictured.
7. **Fine paintbrushes:** for gluing and painting.
8. **Dusting brushes:** for dusting edible lustre dusts on to icing.
9. **Cellophane/acetate sheet:** for 'run-out' icing decorations (see p. 107).
10. **Cocktail sticks (toothpicks):** for colouring and curling icing.
11. **Piping (pastry) bags:** for royal icing decorations.
12. **Piping tubes (tips):** for use with piping (pastry) bags, to pipe royal icing.
13. **Ball tool:** for frilling and thinning the edges of flower paste.
14. **Foam pad:** for softening and frilling flower paste.
15. **Icing smoother:** for smoothing sugarpaste-topped cupcakes to achieve an even surface.

cupcake cases

There are so many lovely cupcake cases available nowadays that will suit just about any occasion. There are generally two types of materials: paper and foil. While there are many more beautiful designs in paper, I prefer to use foil cupcake cases because they tend to be a lot stronger, help preserve the cupcake for longer and look more attractive once the cakes have been baked. Sadly, unless the paper cases are quite dark or made with good-quality paper, they tend to become dull and transparent in time.

classic

romance

secret admirer

These rather indulgent chocolate cupcakes instantly evoke the romance and mystery of a glamorous masked ball. With their golden swirled masks, delicate red roses and sumptuous chocolate ganache topping, they are guaranteed to delight and impress. The luxurious mask is simply cut from caramel-coloured flower paste, using the template on p. 118. Brown cupcake cases with gold metallic detail complement the colour scheme and bring a touch of style to the cakes. These masked beauties are the perfect way to reveal your identity to that special somebody you've been admiring from afar.

To add detail to the mask, tassels are carefully cut from the flower paste and decorations are added using piped royal icing. The masks are dusted with gold lustre for a sparkling finishing touch.

you will need

- ♡ cupcakes baked in brown and gold metallic high tea paper cases
- ♡ caramel-coloured flower paste
- ♡ gold edible lustre dust
- ♡ ganache
- ♡ caramel-coloured royal icing
- ♡ clear alcohol
- ♡ small red rolled roses with two extra petals
- ♡ small single red petals
- ♡ mask template (see p. 118)
- ♡ small piping (pastry) bag and tube (tip) no. 1
- ♡ edible glue

1 Roll out the caramel-coloured flower paste until it is 2–3mm (1⁄16–1⁄8in) thick. Using the template on p. 118 as a guide, cut out the masks with a sharp knife. Brush with gold edible lustre dust using a dusting brush and set aside to dry over some kitchen paper (paper towels) arranged in the shape of the mask. Set aside to harden.

2 Spread the ganache on to the cupcakes using a small palette knife, creating a slight dome in the centre of each.

3 Place a no. 1 tube (tip) in the small piping (pastry) bag and fill with caramel-coloured royal icing. Pipe the detail on to the masks using the photo on p. 13 as a guide.

You could easily replace the rich ganache with chocolate buttercream if you prefer.

4 When the piping is dry, paint over the detail with gold edible lustre dust mixed with clear alcohol. Place the mask on the ganache topping.

5 Thinly roll out some more caramel-coloured flower paste, dust it with gold edible lustre dust and cut very thin strips for the tassels on either side of the mask. Stick them carefully in place with some edible glue.

6 Finish by making a couple of small red rolled roses with two extra petals for each cupcake and some single red petals for scattering, following the instructions on p. 112. Arrange them around the mask as desired.

The red rolled roses give the cupcakes a traditional romantic feel. Simply follow the instructions on p. 112 to make.

As an alternative to the mask design, or to mix in with the mask cupcakes, decorate with just three red roses

back to basics flower paste p. 94 ... ganache p. 90 ... royal icing p. 92 ... roses p. 112 ...

classic romance

Beautiful red roses are a classic symbol of love and romance. These simple yet elegant cupcakes are the perfect way to give your heart to that special someone. For an unusual twist, why not vary the colour of the rose to a deep purple or blue?

you will need

- ♡ cupcakes baked in red foil cases
- ♡ buttercream or topping of your choice
- ♡ red roses
- ♡ red edible glitter
- ♡ large piping (pastry) bag and large star tube (tip)
- ♡ edible glue
- ♡ black filigree cupcake wrappers

1 Snip the end off the large piping (pastry) bag and put the star tube (tip) inside. Fill with the buttercream and, holding each cupcake in one hand in turn, pipe a swirl, as shown on p. 99.

2 Create the roses following the instructions on p. 110. Brush lightly with edible glue and sprinkle with red glitter. Leave to dry for a few minutes.

3 Push the roses into the buttercream, then finish by wrapping a black filigree cupcake wrapper around each cupcake.

back to basics buttercream p. 88 … roses p. 110 …

lovebirds

These cute little lovebird cupcakes would make a lovely alternative to a more traditional wedding cake or could be given as favours to really impress your guests.

you will need

- ♡ dome-shaped cupcakes baked in brown foil cases
- ♡ apricot masking jam
- ♡ ivory fondant icing
- ♡ run-out caramel bird decorations (template on p. 118)
- ♡ gold edible lustre dust
- ♡ royal icing
- ♡ dark brown food colour
- ♡ pink folded blossoms
- ♡ small piping (pastry) bag
- ♡ edible glue

1 Boil the apricot masking jam and brush a thin layer over the cupcakes. Chill in the refrigerator until the cupcakes are firm.

2 Dip the cupcakes in the prepared ivory fondant icing, as described on p. 103. Create the caramel-coloured 'run-out' bird decorations following the instructions on p. 107. Brush the birds with gold edible lustre dust.

3 When the fondant has set, colour the royal icing dark brown and fill the piping (pastry) bag. Snip a small hole in the end of the bag and pipe branches on to each cupcake to resemble a tree.

4 Before the icing dries attach the two lovebirds to the cupcakes so that they face each other. Place one lovebird slightly higher than the other.

5 Dot the pink blossoms on to the branches. Use some more royal icing to stick the blossoms on to the branches if they have started to dry out.

Make the run-out birds and folded blossoms in advance, and store them in a cool, dry place

back to basics fondant icing p. 91 … run-outs p. 107 … royal icing p. 92 … blossoms p. 109 …

wedgwood rose

Delicately decorated in their distinctive whites and blues, these cupcakes beautifully display the elegance and romance of the traditional Wedgwood style.

you will need

- dome-shaped cupcakes baked in silver foil cases
- buttercream
- wedgwood blue sugarpaste
- white flower paste
- white rolled roses
- small semi-dry white folded blossoms
- five-petal blossom cutter
- silicone drape and tassel mould
- edible glue

1 Spread a thin layer of buttercream over the cupcakes and chill in the refrigerator until firm. Roll out the blue sugarpaste until it is approximately 4mm (⅛in) thick and cover the cupcakes, as shown on p. 102.

for the roses

2 Roll out some white flower paste and cut out blossoms with the five-petal blossom cutter – you will need one blossom for each rose. Place them on a foam pad and soften the edges using a ball tool. Cup the petals around the rose and set them aside to dry for a few minutes.

3 Arrange the three roses on each cake.

for the edge decoration

4 Cut thin strips from white flower paste and create two loops from each side to form a bow shape, as shown on p. 113. Use the drape mould to make the tassel, as described on p. 114, and attach to the centre of the bow using edible glue. You will need six bows per cupcake.

5 Attach the bows to the cupcakes at equal distances apart using edible glue or royal icing. Fill in the spaces with the small white folded blossoms.

back to basics sugarpaste p. 93 ... flower paste p. 94 ... roses p. 112 ... bows p. 113 ... moulds p. 114 ... blossoms p. 109 ...

city of love

Whisk your true love away to arguably the most romantic city in the world with these Parisian-style cupcakes, each with their own miniature Eiffel tower!

you will need

♡ slightly dome-shaped cupcakes baked in red and white spotty cases

♡ grey soft-peak royal icing

♡ silver edible glitter

♡ buttercream

♡ white sugarpaste

♡ black flower paste

♡ small piping (pastry) bag and tube (tip) no. 1

♡ eiffel tower template (see p. 118)

♡ acetate sheet, lightly greased with white fat (shortening)

♡ edible glue

1 Snip the tip off the small piping (pastry) bag and insert tube (tip) no. 1 before filling it with some grey soft-peak royal icing.

2 Place the Eiffel tower template (see p. 118) under the sheet of acetate and pipe over the lines until you have completed the tower. Working quickly, sprinkle over the silver edible glitter while the icing is still wet so that it sticks easily. Set aside to dry for a few hours.

3 Spread a thin layer of buttercream over the cupcakes and chill in the refrigerator until firm.

4 Roll out the sugarpaste until it is approximately 4mm (⅛in) thick and cover the cupcakes, as shown on p. 102.

5 Roll out some black flower paste to make the bow, as shown on p. 113. Cut a 'V' shape in the end of both tails with a pair of scissors or a sharp knife.

6 Finish by attaching the Eiffel Tower to the centre of the bow, using a small amount of royal icing.

It's always a good idea to make more Eiffel towers than you require, to allow for any breakages

back to basics royal icing p. 92 :: buttercream p. 88 :: sugarpaste p. 93 :: flower paste p. 94 :: bows p. 113

very vintage

beautiful birdcage

Vintage or garden-style weddings are often decorated with gorgeous little birdcages and these striking cupcakes reflect this theme. The bird and cage are assembled from white flower paste, with a little help from some cutters; a process that is surprisingly simple but gives impressive results. Pretty blossoms scattered around the cage enhance the vintage, romantic feel and can even be coloured to complement the bridal colour scheme. These beautiful cupcakes would make perfect wedding favours.

White doves are a traditional symbol of peace, love, faith and fidelity, which makes them the ideal decoration for this bridal cupcake. The bird is simply modelled from flower paste, using cutters for the wings and tail.

you will need

- ♡ dome-shaped cupcakes baked in silver foil cases
- ♡ buttercream
- ♡ dusky blue sugarpaste
- ♡ white flower paste
- ♡ green flower paste
- ♡ white royal icing
- ♡ pink folded blossoms
- ♡ icing smoother
- ♡ edible glue
- ♡ cocktail sticks (toothpicks)
- ♡ small teardrop cutters: approx. 7.5mm (¼in) and slightly larger
- ♡ cake dummy
- ♡ small piping (pastry) bag and tube (tip) no. 1.5

covering the cupcakes

1 Spread a thin layer of buttercream over the cupcakes and chill in the refrigerator until firm.

2 Roll out the sugarpaste until it is approximately 4mm (⅛in) thick and cover the cupcakes, as shown on p. 102.

for the cage

3 Roll out very thin sausage shapes of white flower paste to make the bars of the cage, using the icing smoother to create a smooth surface. You will need at least six pieces, each about 6–7.5cm (2½–3in) long.

4 Brush a little edible glue on to the cupcakes and stick the bars in place, spacing them evenly apart around the cakes. Join them neatly where they meet in the middle and trim away any excess paste where it hangs over the sides of the cupcake.

5 Using a ball tool, make a small dip in the middle where the bars meet. Roll a small ball of flower paste, flatten it and gently press it into the little hole, making another indentation in the top.

6 Roll another thin sausage shape, again about 6–7.5cm (2½–3in) long, to make the loop on the top of the cake. Bend the two ends round to meet each other and press the hook into the hole in the centre of the cupcake, securing it in place with a little edible glue.

The white cage bars stand out beautifully against the dusky blue covering, enhancing the vintage feel.

for the bird

7 Start by rolling a small marble-sized ball of white flower paste and shaping it into a cone shape for the bird's body. Roll a pea-sized ball for the head and make a tiny triangular piece for the beak. Attach in place with some edible glue.

8 To make the wings and tail, cut out teardrop shapes using the cutters. You will need four small teardrops and one slightly larger one per bird. Stick two smaller teardrops either side of the larger one to make the bird's tail. The two remaining teardrops are for the bird's wings. Set the birds aside for 30 minutes or so to dry.

9 Stick the birds on to the cupcakes using a small amount of royal icing. Cut some more teardrop shapes from thinly rolled-out green flower paste to form the leaves and attach them to the cupcakes with the blossoms.

to finish

10 Use the small piping (pastry) bag with a no. 1.5 tube (tip) and white royal icing to pipe a snail trail border around the edge of the cupcakes, as shown on p. 106.

The folded blossoms are so pretty and very simple to make, following the instructions on p. 109.

Insert a cocktail stick (toothpick) into the underside of the bird's body so that you can hold and build it without damaging it, then set in a cake dummy to dry

back to basics buttercream p. 83 ... sugarpaste p. 93 ... flower paste p. 94 ... blossoms p. 109 ... royal icing p. 92 ...

vintage chic

This design has been inspired by one of my favourite fabric designers, Cath Kidston, who specializes in creating very pretty vintage floral prints.

you will need

- ♡ dome-shaped cupcakes baked in silver foil cases
- ♡ apricot masking jam
- ♡ green fondant icing
- ♡ white sugarpaste
- ♡ paste food colours: pink, claret, green
- ♡ very soft-peak royal icing
- ♡ large six-petal blossom cutter or cookie cutter
- ♡ edible glue
- ♡ rose embosser
- ♡ small piping (pastry) bag and tube (tip) no. 0

1 Boil the apricot masking jam and brush a thin layer on to the cupcakes. Chill the cupcakes in the refrigerator until they are firm.

2 Dip the cupcakes in the prepared different-coloured fondant icings, as shown on p. 103.

3 Roll out the white sugarpaste fairly thinly and cut out the large blossom shape, sticking it on to the centre of the cupcake with a tiny amount of edible glue. Very lightly press the embosser into the sugarpaste to make the basic outline of the rose.

4 Dilute some of the pink and claret paste colours with some water and start to paint the rose. Water down some green food colour and apply it in the same way to paint in the leaves. You will need to paint in extra leaves without an outline as a guide around the top of the rose.

5 Finish the cupcake by piping little dots around the blossom with white royal icing using a piping (pastry) bag with a no. 0 tube (tip), as shown on p. 106.

By using different paste strengths or colours you can make the rose look more realistic

---

back to basics fondant icing p. 91 … royal icing p. 92 … sugarpaste p. 93 …

cameo flowers

Cameos are becoming really fashionable again and it's easy to replicate these gorgeous little art pieces in sugar using a sugarcraft mould.

you will need

- ♡ cupcakes baked in black paper cases
- ♡ flower paste: cream, black, grey
- ♡ grey royal icing
- ♡ silver edible lustre dust
- ♡ clear alcohol
- ♡ vanilla buttercream
- ♡ cameo flower mould (FI)
- ♡ white fat (shortening)
- ♡ wax paper
- ♡ small circle cutter
- ♡ edible glue
- ♡ small piping (pastry) bag and tube (tip) no. 1
- ♡ large piping (pastry) bag and large star tube (tip)

1 Lightly grease the cameo flower mould with white fat (shortening) and press a small amount of cream flower paste into the flower part of the mould only. You may need to roll up several small pieces of flower paste to do this.

2 Fill the rest of the mould with black flower paste. Use a sharp knife to cut away any excess paste so that the inner indented area is flat. Turn the mould out on to some wax paper.

3 Thinly roll out some grey flower paste and cut out ten small circles. Place the circles around the oval cameo, tucking half of the circle underneath. Stick the circles in place, one at a time, using some edible glue.

4 Using the grey royal icing and tube (tip) no. 1, pipe one dot in between each circle and three dots against the cameo on each circle, as shown on p. 106. Pipe an additional two outer dots on each circle. Leave to dry completely for a few hours or overnight.

5 Carefully paint the dots with silver lustre dust, using only a small amount of clear alcohol – if you make the royal icing too wet, it will start to dissolve.

6 Snip the end off the large piping (pastry) bag and place the star tube (tip) inside. Fill with the buttercream and, holding each cupcake in one hand in turn, pipe a swirl, as shown on p. 99.

7 Place the cameos on the buttercream swirls. Make small black bows as described on p. 113 and place beneath the cameos on the cupcakes.

back to basics flower paste p. 94 ... moulds p. 114 ... royal icing p. 92 ... buttercream p. 88 ... bows p. 113 ...

pretty pearls

Adorn your cupcakes with pretty pearls for a vintage look. These daintily decorated cupcakes would be perfect for a girly celebration such as a bridal shower.

you will need

♡ dome-shaped cupcakes baked in gold cases, either dipped in fondant icing or covered with sugarpaste

♡ flower paste: dusky peachy-pink, cream, caramel

♡ edible lustre dust: pearl white, gold

♡ pearl dragees

♡ royal icing

♡ edible glue

♡ perfect pearls mould (FI)

♡ white fat (shortening)

♡ five-petal blossom cutters in two sizes

1 Thinly roll out the peachy-pink flower paste to a circle approximately 13cm (5in) in diameter. Tuck the edges underneath all the way around and gather the flower paste up loosely to resemble a piece of fabric. Attach to the cupcake using a small amount of edible glue.

2 Grease the small and medium moulds lightly with a small amount of white fat (shortening). Roll a thin sausage shape with the cream flower paste to about 15cm (6in) long and press it into the medium pearl mould. Trim any excess paste with a small sharp knife, then remove the pearls from the mould and dust with the pearl white lustre dust. Repeat for the smaller pearls.

3 Lay the two strings of pearls over the cupcake and join them to make a double pearl bracelet. Attach this carefully in place using edible glue. The join will need to be underneath the flower decoration.

4 Use the cutters to cut out two different sizes of blossoms from thinly rolled caramel-coloured flower paste. Soften the edges on a foam pad using a ball tool. Brush them with gold lustre dust and stick them together. Dab a small amount of edible glue in the centre of each flower and stick down seven pearl dragees: one in the centre and the other six surrounding it. Attach the flower over the join in the pearls using a dab of royal icing and then set aside to dry.

back to basics fondant icing p. 91 ... sugarpaste p. 93 ... flower paste p. 94 ... moulds p. 114 ... blossoms p. 108 ...

floral lace

This delicate design has been inspired by vintage wedding dresses. By pressing textured material into the cut flowers, it's easy to create a lacy, fabric-like effect.

you will need

♡ dome-shaped cupcakes baked in blue foil cases, covered with ivory sugarpaste

♡ ivory flower paste

♡ ivory royal icing

♡ selection of blossom cutters

♡ textured materials, e.g. lace, netting or textured rolling pins

♡ edible glue

♡ small piping (pastry) bag and tube (tip) no. 1

1 Cut out the larger blossoms from some thinly rolled-out flower paste to form the outer parts of the flower. Press some textured material into the cut blossoms and soften the edges of the flowers on a foam pad with a ball tool to give them some shape. Set aside to dry a little for a few minutes.

2 Attach the flowers in a random fashion using royal icing. Snip the end off the piping (pastry) bag and place the no. 1 tube (tip) inside. Fill the bag with royal icing and pipe an outline around the edge of the flowers (see p. 106).

3 Repeat the first two steps to make the smaller blossoms. Stick them inside the larger flowers on the cupcakes with some royal icing. Some have three layers, while the medium-sized flowers have only two. You will need to pipe the outlines around the flowers before you stick the next layer on top.

4 To make the flowers that are stuck flat against the cupcakes, repeat the method for step 1 but without softening the edges of the paste. Attach these in a random fashion to the cupcakes in and among the larger blossoms using edible glue. You will need enough flowers to cover most of the surface of the cupcake. Pipe the outline around the edge of the flowers as before.

5 Pipe little dots in the centres of the raised flowers only (see p. 106). Pipe three dots for the smaller flowers and five or six dots for the larger ones.

6 Finish by piping a snail trail border around the edge of the cupcake, as shown on p. 106.

back to basics sugarpaste p. 93 ... flower paste p. 94 ... blossoms p. 108 ... royal icing p. 92 ...

art from
the heart

retro hearts

These fun and funky cupcakes are really quick and easy to make and would suit a less formal occasion such as a hen party or engagement. Chocolate cupcakes are topped with a swirl of sweet chocolate buttercream and finished with a colourful flower paste heart that can be decorated in any way you choose. The hearts are finished with a coating of gold lustre dust to give them a touch of glitz and glamour and to enhance the retro feel. These cupcakes are guaranteed to make a statement.

The hearts are simply cut from flower paste using cookie cutters and then decorated using shapes in contrasting colours. Whether you choose spots or hearts, make sure your design is as bright and bold as possible.

you will need

♡ cupcakes baked in brown foil cases

♡ flower paste: pale pink, deep pink, blue, caramel

♡ gold edible lustre dust

♡ clear alcohol

♡ chocolate buttercream

♡ small heart-shaped cookie cutters: 4.5cm and 3cm (1¾in and 1¼in) wide

♡ small heart cutter, 1.5cm (⅝in) wide

♡ small circle cutter, 5mm (¼in)

♡ edible glue

♡ large piping (pastry) bag and large star tube (tip)

decorating the hearts

1 Cut out hearts from each of the coloured flower pastes using the largest heart-shaped cookie cutters.
2 For the triple heart decoration, repeat step 1 using smaller heart-shaped cutters and layer the smaller hearts in place using edible glue.

3 For the dot decoration, choose one of the hearts and cut circles from the caramel-coloured flower paste. Stick them on to the heart in a random fashion with some edible glue. Trim any circles that overlap the edge of the heart with a small sharp knife. You can repeat this using different colour combinations.

The hearts can easily be made in advance and stored in a box

Decorate the hearts in any way you desire. You could even add stripes by cutting strips of flower paste in various colours and attaching them to the hearts using edible glue.

covering the cupcakes

4 Paint the caramel flower paste with gold lustre dust made into a paste by mixing with some clear alcohol.

5 Snip the end off the large piping (pastry) bag and place the star tube (tip) inside. Fill the bag with the chocolate buttercream and pipe a big swirl on top of the cupcake, as shown on p. 99. Finish by placing the colourful flower paste hearts at an angle on the cupcakes.

Use vanilla buttercream instead as a neutral background and choose any colour scheme you fancy, to suit the occasion

The chocolate buttercream topping can be replaced with a rich ganache swirl if you prefer (see p. 90).

back to basics flower paste p. 94 ... buttercream p. 88 ..

french toile

These charming cupcakes are beautifully decorated in the style of French toile fabric – ideal for a romantic country wedding or a birthday celebration.

you will need

- ♡ slightly dome-shaped cupcakes baked in silver foil cases
- ♡ buttercream
- ♡ ivory sugarpaste
- ♡ royal icing: grey, ivory
- ♡ black paste food colour
- ♡ french toile stencil (DS)
- ♡ circle cutter slightly larger than the top of the cupcake, approx. 6cm (2½in)
- ♡ icing smoother
- ♡ small piping (pastry) bag and tube (tip) no. 1

1 Spread a thin layer of buttercream over the cupcakes and chill in the refrigerator for about 15 minutes.

2 It's best to work on one cupcake at a time, so only roll out about 100g (3½oz) ivory sugarpaste to begin with, until it is about 4mm (⅛in) thick.

3 Choose one of the designs on the stencil and place it over the sugarpaste. Gently hold the stencil down on the sugarpaste and, using a small palette knife, smear the grey royal icing across the top to mark the design.

4 Carefully lift the stencil away, cut out around the design with the circle cutter and place the sugarpaste circle on top of the cupcake using a palette knife or sharp knife. Gently smooth down the edges using an icing smoother, as described on p. 102, being careful not to smudge the stencil decoration. If you do have any accidents, use a small sharp knife to scrape away any smudging.

5 Water down some black food colour and shade in lowlights so that the stencil design has more definition.

6 Finish by piping a snail trail border around the edge of the cupcake with ivory royal icing, as shown on p. 106.

Choose a design that will fit easily within the circumference of the top of the cupcake

back to basics buttercream p. 88 … sugarpaste p. 93 … royal icing p. 92 …

rococo revival

These ornate-looking cupcakes are so luxurious, and with their elegant golden swirls in a bright and bold rococo style, they are sure to stand out from the crowd.

you will need

- ♡ dome-shaped cupcakes baked in gold foil cases
- ♡ apricot masking jam
- ♡ turquoise fondant icing
- ♡ royal icing: caramel, green
- ♡ edible lustre dust: gold, pink
- ♡ clear alcohol
- ♡ small piping (pastry) bags and tube (tip) no. 1
- ♡ pink rolled roses with two extra inner petals and three extra outer petals

1 Boil the apricot masking jam and brush a thin layer on to the cupcakes. Chill the cupcakes in the refrigerator until they are firm.

2 Dip the cupcakes in the coloured fondant, as shown on p. 103.

3 Snip the end off a small piping (pastry) bag and insert the no. 1 tube (tip). Fill the bag with caramel-coloured royal icing. Mark four points on the cupcake to show the end of the inner scrolls that curve to the left. Mark another four points towards the edge of the cupcake, in between the inner four points to show where the inner scroll will finish.

4 Pipe the four inner swirls on to the cupcake, trying to make them the same shape and size. If you make a mistake, wait a minute or so for the icing to dry and carefully scrape it off with a sharp knife.

5 Pipe the scrolls that curl to the right in between the scrolls you have just completed, then pipe in the little leaf-shaped details. Once the icing is completely dry, mix the gold edible lustre dust with some clear alcohol and paint over the scrolls.

6 Dust the pink roses with pink edible lustre dust and stick them on to the cupcakes with some royal icing. Cut a small inward 'V' shape in another piping (pastry) bag and pipe leaves with stiff green royal icing around the roses.

back to basics fondant icing p. 91 … royal icing p. 92 … roses p. 112 …

confetti charm

These cupcakes are really pretty and so quick to make – perfect when you are short of time or need to make a large batch for an occasion such as a wedding or anniversary party.

you will need

- ♡ cupcakes baked in red foil cases
- ♡ red flower paste
- ♡ pink edible lustre dust
- ♡ buttercream or topping of your choice
- ♡ pink lustre heart sprinkles
- ♡ small heart cutter, 1.5cm (⅝in)
- ♡ large piping (pastry) bag and large star tube (tip)
- ♡ pink heart cupcake wrapper (optional)

1 Thinly roll out the red flower paste and cut out the hearts using the small heart cutter. Brush them with the pink edible lustre dust.

2 Snip the end off the piping (pastry) bag and place the star tube (tip) inside. Fill the bag with the buttercream and, holding each cupcake in one hand in turn, pipe a swirl, as shown on p. 99.

3 Decorate the cupcakes with the cut-out hearts and sprinkle over the pink lustre heart sprinkles. Finish by wrapping each cupcake in a pink heart cupcake wrapper, if desired.

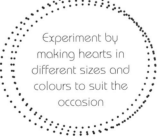

Experiment by making hearts in different sizes and colours to suit the occasion

back to basics flower paste p. 94… buttercream p. 88 …

lacy wonder

It's hard to believe that these beautiful lacy decorations are simply made from silicone moulds! They are so pretty and dainty, and would complement a bridal theme to perfection.

you will need

- ♡ dome-shaped cupcakes baked in gold foil cases, covered with ivory-coloured sugarpaste
- ♡ cream flower paste
- ♡ ivory pearl edible lustre dust
- ♡ ivory ruffled rolled roses
- ♡ ivory royal icing
- ♡ lace-maker heart mould (CK)
- ♡ lace-maker scallop border mould (CK)
- ♡ edible glue

1 Thinly roll out some cream flower paste. Dust both parts of the heart-shaped mould with ivory pearl edible lustre dust and press the flower paste top-side down into the bottom part of the mould.

2 Press the top piece of the mould into the bottom piece with the flower paste in between. Carefully tear away the excess paste around the lace shape while pressing down firmly on the top of the mould.

3 Remove the flower paste from the mould. You may need to use a sharp knife to avoid tearing the flower paste. Brush the piece of icing with extra lustre dust if necessary. Attach the heart to the centre of the cupcake using edible glue.

4 Roll out a long, thin piece of flower paste and cut a 2.5cm (1in) wide strip to fit around the top of the cupcake (approximately 18cm/7in in length).

5 Repeat steps 1–3 but using the border mould and attach the border around the cupcake with some edible glue.

6 Finish by sticking three little ivory rolled roses with ruffled petals to the centre of the heart with ivory royal icing.

back to basics sugarpaste p. 93 ... flower paste p. 94 ... moulds p. 114 ... roses p. 112 ...

flowers
with love

forget-me-not

Fall in love with this stunning design featuring a delicate butterfly resting among an array of gorgeous blue forget-me-nots. The butterfly is created using watered-down royal icing to make two 'run-out' wings, joined together with soft-peak piped icing. The crisp white of the royal icing stands out strikingly against the pale blue of the forget-me-nots, which is complemented beautifully by the blue foil cupcake cases. These cupcakes would make a perfect gift to show your mum that you care on Mother's Day, or to celebrate a cherished Grandmother's birthday.

Follow the instructions on p. 108 to create the forget-me-nots. To make them look really abundant, it's important to create a large number of blossoms and attach them as close together as possible, sticking some on top of others for height.

you will need

- ♡ dome-shaped cupcakes baked in blue foil cases, either dipped in white fondant or covered with sugarpaste
- ♡ run-out white butterfly wing decorations (template on p. 118)
- ♡ white royal icing
- ♡ small pale blue blossoms
- ♡ edible lustre dust: royal blue, pale blue
- ♡ food colours: yellow, brown
- ♡ wax paper
- ♡ concertina-folded card
- ♡ small piping (pastry) bags and tubes (tips) no. 1 and 0
- ♡ blossom veiner

for the butterfly

1 Create the white butterfly wing 'run-out' decorations using the template on p. 118 at least 8–12 hours in advance, as described on p. 107.

2 To assemble the butterflies, make a fold down a strip of wax paper and put it into a fold of a piece of concertina-folded card. Put some white royal icing into a small piping (pastry) bag with a no. 1 tube (tip). Pipe a short line about 1cm (⅜in) long down the centre of the paper and stick the two 'run-out' wing shapes together. Pipe the head and body of the butterfly and leave to dry completely before removing it from the paper.

Make sure the butterfly is made well in advance of the cupcakes in order for it to set nicely.

for the blossoms

3 Dust the blossoms with the blue edible lustre dusts, brushing some more heavily than others so that they are all slightly different shades.

4 Stick the small blue blossoms all over the cupcake with some white royal icing, starting from the outside and working towards the centre. Stick some of the blossoms on top of each other in the centre of the cupcake to create height.

5 Colour some royal icing yellow and fill a piping (pastry) bag with a no. 0 tube (tip). Pipe six little dots in a circle in the centre of each blossom, leaving a little space in the centre (see p. 106).

6 Colour some more royal icing brown and fill another piping (pastry) bag with the no. 0 tube (tip). Pipe a single tiny dot in the centre of each flower, in the gap between the yellow dots.

Check the consistency of your icing and adjust as necessary — you need to be able to pipe dots, not pointed cones

7 Carefully attach the butterfly to the top of the blossoms using a small amount of stiff white royal icing. You may need to rest the wings slightly against the blossoms to give them extra support.

If you prefer, you could make the blossoms in a variety of colours to suit the occasion.

back to basics fondant icing p. 91 ... sugarpaste p. 93 ... run-outs p. 107 ... royal icing p. 92 ... blossoms p. 108 ...

spring blossom

These pretty little cupcakes pick up on the fresh beauty of the spring and would be a perfect way to celebrate a springtime birthday.

you will need

- ♡ cupcakes baked in white paper cases
- ♡ flower paste: white, pale pink
- ♡ pink edible lustre dust
- ♡ buttercream
- ♡ mint green food colour
- ♡ deep pink royal icing
- ♡ assorted five-petal blossom cutters
- ♡ hydrangea or blossom veiner (SS)
- ♡ large piping (pastry) bag and large plain tube (tip)
- ♡ small piping (pastry) bag and tube (tip) no. 1
- ♡ blossom cupcake wrapper (optional)

1 Roll out the white flower paste thinly and use the cutters to cut out the blossoms, as shown on p. 108. Press them between the veiner and sit them in crumpled foil so that they keep their cupped shape as they dry. Repeat using the pale pink flower paste.

2 Dust the centres of the flowers with pink edible lustre dust, dusting some of them more heavily than others. You can also dust some of the petals of the flowers.

3 Colour the buttercream with a small amount of mint green food colour until you have a fresh, spring green colour.

4 Snip off the end of the large piping (pastry) bag and insert the plain tube (tip). Fill the bag with the buttercream and, holding each cupcake in one hand in turn, pipe a swirl, as shown on p. 99.

5 Randomly scatter the blossoms over the cupcakes – you will need about four or five per cake. Pipe small dots in the centre of each flower using the deep pink-coloured royal icing in the small piping (pastry) bag with the tube (tip) no. 1 (see p. 106).

6 Finish by wrapping a white blossom cupcake wrapper around the cupcake, if desired.

back to basics flower paste p. 94 ... blossoms p. 108 ... buttercream p. 88 ... royal icing p. 92 ...

rose bouquet

For a unique way to give thanks to your loved ones, why not say it with flowers? These sweet little blooms are a great way to say 'thanks a bunch'.

you will need

- ♡ dome-shaped cupcakes baked in gold foil cases, covered with ivory sugarpaste
- ♡ green sugarpaste, CMC and white fat (shortening)
- ♡ rolled roses: peach, pale pink, pink, yellow
- ♡ ivory royal icing
- ♡ pink folded blossoms
- ♡ sugar gun
- ♡ edible glue
- ♡ small piping (pastry) bag and tube (tip) no. 1

1 Knead some of the green sugarpaste with a little CMC (see p. 95), together with enough white fat (shortening) to make the paste fairly elastic so that it can be squeezed out of the sugar gun.

2 Fit the sugar gun with the 14-hole disc and fill it with some of the green paste. Squeeze the rose stems out on to the work surface until they are approximately 3cm (1¼in) in length and cut them away from the gun with a small sharp knife. Carefully using the knife to lift them and stick them on to the cupcake using a small amount of edible glue and placing the tighter end towards the centre of the cake. Tease the stems apart slightly at the bottom end.

3 Stick the rolled roses in place with a small amount of royal icing to form a bouquet shape, alternating the colours of the roses as you do so. If necessary, use some more royal icing to stick the little folded blossoms among the roses to fill in any gaps.

4 Roll some small balls of green sugarpaste, making cone shapes, then flatten slightly to make the leaves. You will need approximately five leaves for each cupcake. Stick them in place using edible glue.

5 Finish by piping a dot border (see p. 106). Pipe one row of dots around the edge of the cupcake. Pipe another row of dots below the first, between the dots and missing out every other one.

back to basics sugarpaste p. 93 … modelling paste p. 95 … roses p. 112 … blossoms p. 109 … royal icing p. 92 …

elegant orchids

Orchids are significant for being a universal symbol of love, beauty, wisdom and thoughtfulness. These delicate cupcakes are the perfect way to show that you care.

you will need

- ♡ dome-shaped cupcakes baked in purple and dusky pink foil cases
- ♡ white flower paste
- ♡ apricot masking jam
- ♡ purple tinted and pink fondant icing
- ♡ edible lustre dust: purple, deep pink
- ♡ white royal icing
- ♡ food colours: claret, purple
- ♡ singapore orchid cutters/veiners (HH)
- ♡ edible glue
- ♡ small piping (pastry) bag and tube (tip) no. 1

1 Press a small amount of flower paste into the column mould and remove the shaped piece with a cocktail stick (toothpick). You may need to grease the mould beforehand. Set aside to dry for 20 minutes while you make a few more.

2 Thinly roll out a small amount of flower paste and cut out the trumpet. Place on a foam pad and soften the edges with a ball tool. Wrap the trumpet around the column, securing it in place with edible glue. Tease the centre of the trumpet away from the column. Set aside to dry for an hour or two.

3 Meanwhile, prepare and dip the cupcakes in the fondant, as on p. 103.

4 Roll out the side and tri petals for the orchid and soften the edges with the ball tool as before. Stick one end of each of the two side petals together in the centre of the tri petal. Glue the dry trumpet of the flower on to the five petals with the outer part or the trumpet furthest away from them.

5 Cup and tease the bottom petals around the trumpet to make the orchid. Carefully sit it in a flower former or some crumpled foil until it dries. Brush with the edible lustre dusts and attach to the cupcake using purple tinted royal icing.

6 Colour the royal icing with the food colours (you can vary the shade). Using a small piping (pastry) bag with a no. 1 tube (tip), mark 16 small dots around the cake edge. Pipe from one dot to the next, allowing the icing to fall between them. Pipe a second row below the first, piping little dots either side. Pipe a dot where each point meets. When dry, pipe another dot either side.

back to basics flower paste p. 94 ... fondant icing p. 91 ... royal icing p. 92 ...

daisy delight

The brush embroidery technique here is really simple yet effective to do. Here I have chosen a daisy, but you could use a variety of flowers for stunning effects.

you will need

- ♡ dome-shaped cupcakes baked in brown and gold foil cases
- ♡ buttercream
- ♡ pale yellow sugarpaste
- ♡ white royal icing
- ♡ yellow food colour
- ♡ plunger daisy cutters (PME)
- ♡ small piping (pastry) bags and tube (tip) no. 2 and 1

1 Spread a thin layer of buttercream over the cupcakes and chill in the refrigerator for about 15 minutes.

2 Cover the cupcakes with the yellow sugarpaste, as described on p. 102.

3 Carefully press the cutters into the sugarpaste randomly, while it is still soft, to mark the daisies. Overlap some of the daisies.

4 To carry out the brushwork, place the no. 2 tube (tip) in the piping (pastry) bag and fill it with white royal icing. Pipe around the outline of the daisy and, using a damp fine paintbrush, drag the icing inwards towards the centre of the flower. If you are a beginner, work on half a flower at a time. If there are any thin areas, go over them again with additional royal icing.

5 Repeat this for the other daisies on the cupcake. Where the flowers overlap each other, choose one of them to do the brushwork on so that it looks like the other is underneath it.

6 Colour some royal icing yellow and, using a piping (pastry) bag with a no. 1 tube (tip), pipe small dots for the centres of each flower (see p. 106).

7 Finish by piping a snail trail border around the edge of the cupcake, as shown on p. 106.

back to basics buttercream p. 88 … sugarpaste p. 93 … royal icing p. 92 …

recipes

cupcake recipes

Once you have chosen your cases and have all your equipment to hand, it's time for the fun to begin! In this section you will find a tempting variety of recipes and delicious flavour combinations to try. Most of them can be easily adapted to suit your personal taste (see the individual recipes for suggestions for flavour variations). It's important that your cakes taste as good as they look, so always try to use the finest ingredients you can find.

The recipes that I have included will each make about 12 relatively domed-shaped cupcakes. For some of the projects, a slightly flatter top is required, so you may find you have a little more mixture than necessary. Don't waste it – simply bake more cakes!

I bake all the cupcakes at 170°C/325°F/Gas 3 and most will take about 20 minutes to cook. However, baking time will always vary depending on how full your case is and how efficient your oven is. It's always a good idea to have an oven thermometer to hand just to check the temperature. It's also worthwhile doing a trial batch first, as all ovens behave differently!

tips for perfect cupcakes

- bring all your ingredients to room temperature before mixing your cupcake batter
- accurately measuring your ingredients is vital to cupcake success
- ensure that your cupcake tin is perfectly clean before adding the cases
- check that the cases are sitting perfectly in the pan. Press out any wonky kinks!
- ensure that you don't get any cake batter around the top of the cases as you fill them
- check that your oven is up to temperature before you put the cupcakes in
- turn the cupcakes or swap shelves halfway through the cooking process if your oven doesn't cook very evenly
- the cupcakes are cooked when the mixture springs back when you touch it. Don't overcook them, or they will become dry
- soak the cupcakes with some sugar syrup (see p. 87) when they come out of the oven to enhance the flavour and make them moister
- for best results, cupcakes must be completely cold before decorating

- if you are experimenting with substituting an ingredient, make sure the food item is of a similar texture/consistency
- undecorated cupcakes can usually be frozen for up to a month

classic sponge

This classic recipe is extremely versatile and can be made with numerous flavour variations, some of which I have included below.

you will need

(makes 12 cupcakes)

- ♡ 150g/5½oz unsalted butter, softened
- ♡ 150g/5½oz caster (superfine) sugar
- ♡ ½ tsp/2.5ml vanilla extract
- ♡ 3 medium eggs
- ♡ 150g/5½oz self-raising (-rising) flour
- ♡ flavoured syrup (see p. 87)

1 Preheat your oven to 170°C/325°F/Gas 3.

2 Line the cupcake tin with cupcake cases.

3 In a large electric mixer, beat the butter and sugar together with the vanilla extract until the mixture becomes light and fluffy.

4 Add the eggs gradually, beating well between each addition.

5 Sift the flour, add to the mixture and mix carefully until just combined.

6 Remove the mixing bowl from the mixer and fold the mixture gently through with a spatula. Evenly spoon or pipe the mixture into the cases.

7 Bake the cupcakes in the oven for approximately 20 minutes or until a skewer inserted into the centre of one of the cupcakes comes out clean.

8 Brush the cakes with syrup and allow to cool in the tin for 10 minutes before turning out on to a wire rack to cool completely.

9 Soak the cakes in the flavoured syrup, if desired.

flavour variations

lemon: add the finely grated zest of one unwaxed lemon

orange: add the finely grated zest of one orange

chocolate: replace 10g/¼oz flour with 10g/¼oz cocoa powder (unsweetened cocoa) per 100g/3½oz flour.

chocolate temptation

This mouth-watering recipe is extremely quick and easy to make and has a lovely light texture. Use a chocolate ganache topping rather than buttercream for a richer, more indulgent flavour.

you will need

(makes 12 cupcakes)

- ♡ 100g/3½oz slightly salted butter, softened
- ♡ 220g/7¾oz light brown sugar
- ♡ 1 tsp/5ml vanilla extract
- ♡ 2 medium eggs
- ♡ 160g/5¾oz self-raising (-rising) flour, sifted
- ♡ 40g/1½oz cocoa powder (unsweetened cocoa), sifted
- ♡ 125ml/4 fl oz milk
- ♡ flavoured syrup (see p. 87)

1 Preheat your oven to 170°C/325°F/Gas 3.

2 Line the cupcake tin with cupcake cases.

3 In a large electric mixer, beat the butter and sugar together with the vanilla extract and the eggs until combined.

4 Add the dry ingredients and mix together on a slow speed while adding the milk. Make sure that all the ingredients are mixed together well.

5 Evenly spoon or pipe the mixture into the cases.

6 Bake in the oven for approximately 20 minutes or until a skewer inserted into the centre of one of the cupcakes comes out clean.

7 Brush the cakes with syrup and allow to cool in the tin for 10 minutes before turning out on to a wire rack to cool completely.

8 Soak the cakes in the flavoured syrup, if desired.

flavour variations

chocolate orange: add the finely grated zest of one orange

mocha: add one shot of espresso

carrot and pecan

Grated carrot and chopped nuts give this recipe a lovely texture as well as a divine taste. A lemon topping complements the sponge cake perfectly.

you will need

(makes 12 cupcakes)

- ♡ 125g/4½oz dark brown sugar
- ♡ 125ml/4fl oz vegetable oil
- ♡ 2 medium eggs
- ♡ 190g/6¾oz self-raising (-rising) flour, sifted
- ♡ ¼ tsp bicarbonate of soda (baking soda)
- ♡ 1 tsp mixed spice (apple pie spice)
- ♡ 275g/9½oz grated carrot
- ♡ 60g/2¼oz chopped pecans

1 Preheat your oven to 170°C/325°F/Gas 3.

2 Line the cupcake tin with cupcake cases.

3 In a large electric mixer, beat together the sugar and vegetable oil for about a minute.

4 Add the eggs one at a time, beating well between each addition.

5 Add the dry ingredients and grated carrot alternatively, mixing briefly before each addition.

6 Fold in the chopped pecans.

7 Evenly spoon or pipe the mixture into the cases. Bake in the oven for approximately 20 minutes or until a skewer inserted into the centre of one of the cupcakes comes out clean.

8 Allow the cakes to cool in the tin for 10 minutes before turning out on to a wire rack to cool completely.

flavour variation

carrot and walnut: replace the chopped pecans with 60g/2¼oz chopped walnuts, or any other nut of your choice

rich coffee

Coffee lovers will simply adore this recipe. If you wish, you can make it stronger tasting simply by adding extra coffee and coffee liqueur.

you will need

(makes 12 cupcakes)

- ♡ 2½ tsp coffee granules or 1 double strength shot of espresso
- ♡ 2 tbsp/30ml Tia Maria
- ♡ 4 tbsp/60ml milk
- ♡ 95g/3¼oz unsalted butter, softened
- ♡ 125g/4½oz light brown sugar
- ♡ 2 medium eggs
- ♡ 170g/5¾oz self-raising (-rising) flour, sifted
- ♡ Tia Maria syrup (see p. 87)

1 Preheat your oven to 170°C/325°F/Gas 3.

2 Line the cupcake tin with cupcake cases.

3 Combine the coffee and Tia Maria and then add to the milk. Set aside.

4 In a large electric mixer, beat together the butter and sugar for a minute until the mixture becomes a little paler.

5 Add the eggs one at a time, beating well between each addition.

6 Add half of the flour and half of the coffee mixture and mix until just combined. Add the remaining ingredients in the same way.

7 Evenly spoon or pipe the mixture into the cases.

8 Bake in the oven for approximately 20 minutes or until a skewer inserted into the centre of one of the cupcakes comes out clean.

9 Brush the cakes with syrup and allow to cool in the tin for 10 minutes before turning out on to a wire rack to cool completely.

10 Soak the cakes in the syrup, if desired.

flavour variation

coffee and walnut/hazelnut: replace 20g/¾oz of the flour with the same amount of finely chopped walnuts or hazelnuts

citrus poppyseed

The tangy citrus syrup combined with poppyseeds gives this recipe a lovely moist, interesting texture as well as a delicious flavour.

you will need

(makes 12 cupcakes)

- 1½ tbsp poppyseeds
- 200ml/⅓ pint milk
- 100g/3½oz unsalted butter, softened
- 120g/4¼oz caster (superfine) sugar
- 2 tsp finely grated lemon zest
- 2 tsp finely grated orange zest
- 2 tsp finely grated lime zest
- 2 medium eggs
- 240g/8¾oz self-raising (-rising) flour
- lemon, orange or lime syrup (see p. 87)

1 Preheat your oven to 170°C/325°F/Gas 3.

2 Line the cupcake tin with cupcake cases.

3 Soak the poppyseeds in the milk and set aside for 10 minutes.

4 In a large electric mixer, beat the butter and sugar together with the grated zests until the mixture becomes light and fluffy.

5 Add the eggs one at a time, beating well between each addition.

6 Sift the flour and then add to the mixture, alternating between the milk and poppyseeds. Mix very carefully until just combined.

7 Evenly spoon or pipe the mixture into the cases and bake the cupcakes in the oven for approximately 20 minutes or until a skewer inserted into the centre of one of the cupcakes comes out clean.

8 Brush the cakes fairly heavily with citrus syrup and allow to cool in the tin for 10 minutes before turning out on to a wire rack to cool completely.

flavour variation

simply orange, lemon or lime: add 1 tsp finely grated zest of either orange, lemon or lime

coconut and lime

This delicious recipe brings a touch of the exotic to your baking and is perfect for a tropical wedding or celebration.

you will need

(makes 12 cupcakes)

- 70g/2½oz desiccated (dry unsweetened shredded) coconut
- 100ml/3½fl oz plain yogurt
- 100ml/3½fl oz milk
- 100g/3½oz unsalted butter, softened
- 175g/6oz caster (superfine) sugar
- 1 tbsp finely grated lime zest
- 3 medium eggs
- 210g/7¾oz self-raising (-rising) flour
- lime syrup (see p. 87)

1 Preheat your oven to 170°C/325°F/Gas 3.

2 Line the cupcake tin with cupcake cases.

3 Combine the coconut and yogurt and then add to the milk. Set aside.

4 In a large electric mixer, beat together the butter, sugar and lime zest for a minute or so until the mixture becomes light and fluffy.

5 Add the eggs one at a time, beating well between each addition. Don't worry if the mixture splits here.

6 Add the flour and the yogurt mixture and mix until just combined.

7 Evenly spoon or pipe the mixture into the cases.

8 Bake in the oven for approximately 20 minutes or until a skewer inserted into the centre of one of the cupcakes comes out clean.

9 Brush the cakes with syrup and allow to cool in the tin for 10 minutes before turning out on to a wire rack to cool completely.

10 Soak the cakes in the syrup, if desired.

flavour variation

tropical touch: replace the lime syrup with a Malibu-flavoured syrup

banana and spice

Banana cake is a popular alternative to the more classic recipes and is perfectly complemented by a hint of spice.

you will need

(makes 12 cupcakes)

- 150g/5½oz unsalted butter, softened
- 150g/5½oz light or dark brown sugar
- 3 medium eggs
- 150g/5½oz self-raising (-rising) flour
- ½ tsp mixed spice (apple pie spice)
- 1 large over-ripe banana

1 Preheat your oven to 170°C/325°F/Gas 3.

2 Line the cupcake tin with cupcake cases.

3 In a large electric mixer, beat the butter and sugar together until light and fluffy.

4 Add the eggs gradually, beating well between each addition.

5 Sift the flour with the mixed spice and add to the mixture. Mix very carefully until just combined.

6 Remove the mixing bowl from the mixer, mash the banana and fold it through the mixture gently with a spatula.

7 Evenly spoon or pipe the mixture into the cases and bake in the oven for approximately 20 minutes or until a skewer inserted into the centre of one of the cupcakes comes out clean.

8 Allow the cakes to cool in the tin for 10 minutes before turning out on to a wire rack to cool completely.

Use really over-ripe bananas for a lovely sweet flavour

yogurt, honey and cinnamon

This is a really tasty sweet and spicy recipe. You can experiment with the sweet/spicy combination for the topping until you have a flavour that suits your personal taste.

you will need

(makes 12 cupcakes)

- ♡ 150g/5½oz unsalted butter, softened
- ♡ 135g/4¾oz plain yogurt
- ♡ ½ tsp ground cinnamon
- ♡ 100ml/3½fl oz clear honey
- ♡ 2 medium eggs
- ♡ 40g/1½oz caster (superfine) sugar
- ♡ 195g/7oz self-raising (-rising) flour
- ♡ ½ tsp baking powder
- ♡ honey syrup (see p. 87 – replace 10g/¼oz sugar with 1 tsp/5ml clear honey, or to taste)

1 Preheat your oven to 170°C/325°F/Gas 3.

2 Line the cupcake tin with cupcake cases.

3 In a large electric mixer, beat the butter, yogurt, cinnamon and honey together until the ingredients are all just combined. Transfer to another mixing bowl.

4 Beat the eggs with the sugar using the electric mixer until they are thick and creamy. Combine with the yogurt mixture.

5 Sift the flour and baking powder into the mixture and gently stir until all the ingredients are combined.

6 Evenly spoon or pipe the mixture into the cases.

7 Bake in the oven for approximately 20 minutes or until a skewer inserted into the centre of one of the cupcakes comes out clean.

8 Brush the cakes with syrup and allow to cool in the tin for 10 minutes before turning out on to a wire rack to cool completely.

9 Soak the cupcakes in the syrup, if desired.

These sweet cupcakes are delicious simply decorated with toasted almonds

icing recipes

There are so many ways to decorate cupcakes, from simply dusting with icing (confectioners') sugar and serving with fresh berries, to the more elaborate and decorative designs featuring sugar flowers and intricate piping. As a sugarcrafter, I prefer to cover my cupcakes in either buttercream or ganache, or fondant or sugarpaste, which can all be decorated easily to suit the occasion. Each of these coverings taste unique and will produce different results.

jams and preserves

In addition to the toppings, try experimenting with additional flavours by 'injecting' jams and preserves into your cakes once they have been baked. Simply fill a squeezy bottle with a narrow pointed nozzle with your chosen preserve and insert it carefully into the cupcakes.

sugar syrup

Sugar syrup is brushed on to the cupcakes to add moisture and flavour. Ideally, this should be done while the cupcakes are still warm, to help the syrup soak further into the cakes. The amount of syrup used is a personal choice – if you feel that your cake is quite dry, use more syrup. However, be aware that by adding too much syrup your cake can become too sweet and sticky.

you will need

(for soaking 12 cupcakes)

♡ 75ml/2½fl oz water

♡ 75g/2¾oz caster (superfine) sugar

1 Put the water and sugar into a saucepan and bring to the boil, stirring once or twice.

2 Add any flavouring and allow to cool.

3 Store in an airtight container in the refrigerator for up to one month.

flavoured syrups

vanilla: add 1 tsp/5ml good-quality vanilla extract

lemon: replace the water with freshly squeezed, finely strained lemon juice

orange: replace the water with freshly squeezed, finely strained orange juice

lime: replace the water with freshly squeezed, finely strained lime juice

liqueurs: limoncello, Grand Marnier, Tia Maria and Malibu can also be added to enhance the syrup's flavour

buttercream

This recipe is basically made from butter and icing (confectioners') sugar. I choose not to add milk to my recipes so that the cakes do not need any refrigeration and can be displayed for a longer period of time.

you will need

(for 12 cupcakes)

- 💜 100g/3½oz slightly salted butter, softened
- 💜 200g/7oz icing (confectioners') sugar
- 💜 1 tbsp/15ml water
- 💜 1 tsp/5ml vanilla extract or alternative flavouring (see below)

1 Put the butter and icing (confectioners') sugar into the bowl of an electric mixer and mix together, starting on a low speed to prevent the mixture from going everywhere.

2 Add the water and vanilla extract or other flavouring and increase the speed, beating the buttercream really well until it becomes pale, light and fluffy.

3 Store for up to 2 weeks in an airtight container in the refrigerator.

buttercream flavour variations

citrus: add the finely grated zest of one lemon or orange

lime and malibu: add the finely grated zest of one lime and 1 tsp/5ml Malibu instead of water

coffee: add half a shot of espresso coffee

chocolate: stir in 90g/3¼oz melted white, milk or dark (semisweet) chocolate

passion fruit: stir in 1 tsp/5ml strained and reduced passion fruit pulp

honey: add 1 tsp/5ml clear honey, or to taste

cream cheese frosting

This is a really delicious alternative to buttercream and works really well with the carrot and pecan (see p. 74), coffee (see p. 76), and yogurt, honey and cinnamon (see p. 84) recipes. This frosting does need to be refrigerated until consumption, so you will only be able to decorate your cakes at the last minute. Therefore, I would only use cream cheese frosting as an alternative for the designs covered with buttercream.

you will need

(for 12 cupcakes)

- ♡ 60g/2¼oz unsalted butter, softened
- ♡ 120g/4¼oz cream cheese
- ♡ 1 tsp/5ml vanilla extract or alternative flavouring (see below)
- ♡ 480g/17oz icing (confectioners') sugar

1 Beat the butter, cream cheese and flavouring together until light and fluffy.

2 Gradually add the icing (confectioners') sugar, beating between each addition.

This frosting can be stored for up to 3–4 days in an airtight container in the refrigerator.

flavour variations

lemon: add the finely grated zest of one lemon

lime: add the finely grated zest of one lime

honey: add 1 tbsp/15ml honey, or to taste

coffee: add half a shot of espresso coffee

ganache

Ganache is a rich, smooth filling made from chocolate and cream. It's important to use a good-quality chocolate, with at least 53% cocoa solids, in order to achieve the best result.

you will need

(for 12 cupcakes)

- 200g/7oz dark (semisweet) chocolate, chopped, or callets
- 200g/7oz double (heavy) cream

Try adding a few drops of your favourite liqueur to taste or add ½ tsp/2.5ml liquid glucose to make it extra shiny

1 Place the dark (semisweet) chocolate in a bowl.

2 In a saucepan, bring the cream to the boil, then pour over the chocolate.

3 Stir until the chocolate has all melted and is perfectly mixed in with the cream. Allow to cool and then cover.

4 Store for up to a week in the refrigerator.

fondant icing

Fondant icing is not as indulgent as buttercream and ganache, but is still a lovely sweet covering. This type of fondant is a liquid icing that is heated until it becomes runny enough for you to dip your cupcakes in. The fondant sets when the icing returns to room temperature.

you will need

(for 20 cupcakes)

- ♡ 1kg/2lb 4oz tub ready-made fondant
- ♡ 1 tbsp/15ml liquid glucose
- ♡ 1 quantity sugar syrup (see p. 87)
- ♡ food colouring as required

1 Put the fondant into a microwavable bowl and warm in the microwave for approximately 1½ minutes on medium power until it can be easily poured into your microwavable bowl. Add the glucose and half of the sugar syrup.

2 Gently stir the ingredients together, trying to avoid too many air bubbles. Add any food colouring as desired. If you are dipping the cupcakes into more than one colour of icing, split the fondant between two bowls beforehand. Cover up the bowl you are not using immediately with cling film (plastic wrap).

3 Return the fondant to the microwave and heat it gently until it is quite warm. It should be slightly warmer than body temperature (38–40°C/100.4–104°F) but no hotter. Test the consistency by dipping one of the cupcakes into the fondant. If it's too thick, add more sugar syrup until the fondant coats the cupcake nicely. Be careful not make it too runny or the fondant won't set.

royal icing

Royal icing is used for piped decorations, for stencil work or simply for attaching paste items to your cupcakes.

you will need

(makes 600g/1lb 5oz)

♡ 2 egg whites or 15g/½oz dried egg albumen powder mixed with 75ml/ 2½fl oz water

♡ 500g/1lb 2oz icing (confectioners') sugar

1 If you are using dried egg powder, soak this in water at least 30 minutes in advance, or ideally overnight in the refrigerator.

2 Sift the icing (confectioners') sugar into the mixing bowl of an electric mixer and add the egg whites or strained reconstituted egg mixture.

3 Mix together on a low speed for about 3–4 minutes until the icing has reached a stiff-peak consistency.

4 Store the icing in an airtight container covered with a damp, clean cloth to prevent it from drying out. Royal icing will keep for up to 3 days, but for best results, use it when it is as fresh as possible.

sugarpaste (rolled fondant)

Sugarpaste is a sweet, thick, opaque paste that is soft, pliable, easily coloured and extremely versatile. While you can make your own sugarpaste using the recipe below, I prefer to use ready-made sugarpaste, which is widely available from sugarcraft suppliers (see p. 119) and can be found in most good supermarkets. You will need a small amount of buttercream or ganache (see p. 88 or 90) to attach the sugarpaste to the cupcake.

you will need

(makes 1kg/2¼lb)

- ♡ 4 tbsp/60ml cold water
- ♡ 4 tsp/1 sachet powdered gelatine
- ♡ 125ml/4fl oz liquid glucose
- ♡ 1 tbsp/15ml glycerine
- ♡ 1kg/2¼lb icing (confectioner's) sugar, sifted, plus extra for dusting

1 Place the water in a small bowl, sprinkle over the gelatine and leave to soak until spongy.

2 Stand the bowl over a saucepan of hot, but not boiling, water and stir until the gelatine has dissolved. Add the glucose and glycerine, stirring until well blended and runny.

3 Put the icing (confectioners') sugar in a large bowl. Make a well in the centre and slowly pour in the liquid, stirring constantly. Mix well.

4 Turn out on to a surface dusted with icing (confectioners') sugar and knead until smooth, sprinkling with extra sugar if the paste becomes too sticky. The paste can be used immediately or tightly wrapped and stored in a plastic bag until required

flower paste (petal/gum paste)

Flower paste is a specially formulated sugarpaste developed to be the ideal medium for creating detailed pieces such as sugar flowers. Like sugarpaste, I prefer to use ready-made flower paste, which can be bought from specialist sugarcraft suppliers (see p. 119).

working with flower paste

Flower paste dries quickly, so cut off only as much as you need and reseal the remainder. Work it well with your fingers – it should 'click' between your fingers when it's ready to use. There are several varieties available, so try out a few to see which you prefer.

edible glue

Edible glue can be bought ready-made, but it's easy to make yourself. Add ¼ tsp/1.25ml CMC to 25ml/¾fl oz warm water in a small pot or container. Shake well and leave for a few hours to thicken before use. Store in the refrigerator.

modelling paste

This versatile paste keeps its shape well and dries harder than sugarpaste. Modelling paste can be bought ready-made, but can also be simply made by adding gum tragacanth or CMC to sugarpaste. CMC is a synthetic version of gum tragacanth and will work almost as soon as it is kneaded into the sugarpaste. Gum tragacanth will take at least an hour before it starts to harden. Below is a basic quantity guide, but you may want to add more or less depending on the decoration you are making.

you will need

- ♡ 1 tsp/5ml gum tragacanth or CMC
- ♡ 200g/7oz sugarpaste

1 Knead the gum tragacanth or CMC into the sugarpaste.

2 Keep the modelling paste in a plastic bag until ready to use to prevent it from drying out.

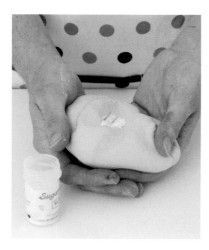

techniques

icing techniques

Once your cupcakes are baked and cooled, it's decoration time! How you choose to decorate your cupcakes is largely a matter of taste and personal preference, but time and quantity will also influence your decision.

preparing the cupcakes

Before you cover the cupcakes, make sure they are completely cool. Brush with extra sugar syrup if you think they might be a bit dry or if you want them to be really moist. Cupcakes topped with buttercream, cream cheese frosting or ganache don't need to be perfectly shaped, as the icing will hide any imperfections. However, cupcakes that are to be covered with sugarpaste and fondant in particular will need to be much smoother and nicely shaped, which can be done by shaving off any lumps and bumps with a sharp serrated knife.

Refrigerate the cakes so that they are chilled and easier to shape

buttercream, cream cheese frosting and ganache

Using these three toppings is the simplest way to decorate your cupcakes. To get each cake looking perfect, you will need a little practice.

You can pipe the topping on using a large plastic piping (pastry) bag, making a peak or swirl with either a plain or star-shaped tube (tip). Alternatively, simply use a palette knife to spread the topping on evenly to create a nice domed top. Make sure your icing is soft when you use it – you may need to re-beat it or to warm it slightly if the room temperature is fairly cold.

to create a swirl

1 Place the piping tube (tip) in a large piping (pastry) bag, then fill half the bag with your chosen topping. Twist the top of the bag to seal.

2 Holding the bag vertically, start at the centre of the cupcake. Apply pressure to the bag and then move the tube (tip) to the edge of the cupcake and around the centre of the cake in an anti-clockwise direction.

3 Once you have completed the circle, continue piping by adding one or two smaller circles of the topping on top of the first.

colouring icing

There are two types of colourings used to colour icing: paste and liquid. I prefer to use paste colours, especially when colouring sugarpaste and flower paste, to prevent the icing from becoming too wet and sticky.

colouring tips

- Liquid colours work well with royal icing and liquid fondant. However, you must be careful not to add too much too soon.
- Be aware that the colour of your icing can often change as it dries – some colours tend to fade, while others darken.
- Always add your colour gradually and keep some extra white icing to hand in case you make a mistake.
- Be careful with pale colours, as only a little colour is needed.
- Deep colours require plenty of colouring and may become sticky. To prevent this, add a pinch of gum tragacanth and leave for an hour or two to make your paste firmer.

colouring sugarpaste

1 Place a little paste colour on the end of a cocktail stick (toothpick), or a larger amount on a palette knife.
2 Add the colour to the paste and knead in thoroughly, adding more until the desired effect is achieved.

colouring fondant

1 Add a small amount of paste or liquid colour to your fondant and stir in with a palette knife.
2 Add additional colouring if required to achieve the desired depth of colour.

covering with sugarpaste

Using sugarpaste is a very quick and contemporary way of decorating cupcakes. You can just cut a circle to fit inside the cupcake case, but I prefer to cover the cake completely and go right up to the edge of the cake. Use cupcakes that have a nice domed shape to them.

1 Using a palette knife, spread a thin layer of flavoured buttercream or ganache over the cake to form a perfectly rounded and smooth surface for the sugarpaste to sit on. Refrigerate for 20 minutes or so until the cupcakes are firm.

2 Knead the sugarpaste until warm and pliable, then roll out to a depth of 5mm/³⁄₁₆in and cut circles slightly bigger than the cupcake. I would suggest cutting out nine at a time. Cover any circles you are not using with cling film (plastic wrap).

3 Drape the sugarpaste circles over the cupcakes one at a time and use an icing smoother to cut away the overhanging paste around the sides. Smooth all the way over and around.

It's a good idea to use spacers when rolling out the sugarpaste, to ensure an even thickness

fondant-dipped cupcakes

This technique is much more involved than the others, but liquid fondant really makes a delicious and great-looking topping. Recipes more suitable for this technique are the classic sponge (see p. 70) and the chocolate temptation cake mixtures (see p. 72). These are light in texture and can be easily shaved into the dome shape required and then dipped into the fondant.

1 Prepare the cupcakes by shaving off any uneven bumps so that they are perfectly smooth and have a lovely domed shape.

2 Brush the cupcakes with some boiled apricot masking jam and refrigerate for at least 15 minutes while you prepare the fondant.

3 Dip the cupcakes one at a time into the fondant. Allow the excess to drip down for a second, then turn the cake up the right way to set. Once you have dipped all the cakes, you will probably need to give them a second coating. Wait 5–10 minutes before doing this, or until the first coat is dry.

decorating techniques

Once you have iced your cupcakes, the fun can really begin. Using royal icing, run-outs and flower paste decorations, you can transform your cupcakes into little masterpieces.

royal icing

Royal icing is such a versatile medium and is used in most of the projects in this book.

making a piping (pastry) bag

1 Cut two equal triangles from a large square piece of parchment paper. As a guide, for small bags cut from 15–20cm (6–8in) square paper and for large bags cut from 30–35cm (12–14in) square paper.

2 Keeping the centre point towards you with the longest side furthest away, curl the right-hand corner inwards and bring the point to meet the centre point. Adjust your hold so that you have the two points together between your right thumb and index finger.

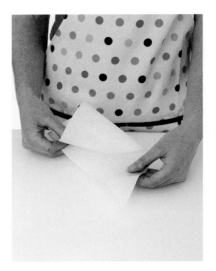

Make lots of piping (pastry) bags at a time and put aside for later use

3 With your left hand, curl the left point inwards, bringing it across the front and around to the back of the other two points in the centre of the cone. Adjust your grip again so that you are now holding the three points together with both your thumbs and index fingers.

4 Tighten the cone-shaped bag by gently rubbing your thumb and index fingers forwards and backwards until you have a sharp tip at the end of the bag.

5 Carefully fold the back of the bag (where all the points meet) inwards, making sure you press hard along the fold. Repeat this to make sure it is really secure.

piping with royal icing

For basic piping work, use soft-peak icing. The size of the tube (tip) will depend on the job at hand and how competent you are. For most projects in this book, I use a no. 1 tube (tip).

1 Fill the piping (pastry) bag until it is no more than one-third full. Fold the top over, away from the join, until you have a tight and well-sealed bag. It's important to hold the bag in the correct way. Use your index finger to guide the bag (you can also use your other hand to guide you if it's easier).

2 Touch the tube (tip) down, then lift the bag up in a smooth movement, squeezing gently. Decrease the pressure and touch it back down to the point where you want the icing to finish. Try not to drag the icing along, or it will become uneven. Use a template as a guide where possible (see p. 118).

3 To pipe dots, squeeze the icing out gently until you have the dot the size you require. Stop squeezing, then lift the bag. If there is a peak in the icing, use a damp brush to flatten it down.

Royal icing can also be used for sticking on decorations and gluing cakes together. Always use stiff icing for this

piping a snail trail border
Squeeze out a large dot of icing and drag the tube (tip) through it to one side. Repeat this continuously around the edge of the cupcake.

run-outs

Royal icing is thinned down with water to make 'run-outs' – smooth-iced, flat decorations that are used for the birds on p. 18, and the butterfly on p. 56. To get the right consistency for your run-outs, test the icing by lifting your spoon and letting the icing drip back into the bowl. The icing falling back into the bowl should remain on the surface for five seconds before disappearing into the rest.

you will need

- ♡ piping (pastry) bags
- ♡ piping tubes (tips)
- ♡ cellophane or a sheet of acetate, lightly greased with white fat (shortening)

1 Fill a small piping (pastry) bag, with a no. 1 tube (tip) inserted, with soft-peak royal icing. Pipe the outline of the shape you require using the templates provided on p. 118.

2 Fill another piping (pastry) bag with 'run-out/flooding' icing, created as described above, and fill the shape in. For filling in the birds, it's best to use a no. 0 tube (tip), as it's quite a finely shaped decoration, but you can use the no. 1 tube (tip) for the butterfly. Leave the decoration to dry completely, ideally overnight, before lifting off the cellophane or acetate sheet.

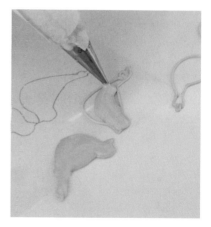

flower paste decorations

Flower paste is used for creating more delicate decorations such as flowers, frills and bows, as it can be rolled out really thinly. Knead the paste well by continuously pulling it apart with your fingers.

blossoms

Blossoms can be made in a variety of shapes and sizes. They can be pressed, frilled and veined to create the shape you desire and need to be left to dry before attaching to the cupcakes.

you will need

♡ flower paste

♡ small non-stick board with non-slip mat

♡ small non-stick rolling pin

♡ blossom cutters

♡ foam pad and ball tool or blossom veiner

♡ crumpled foil or ridged piece of sponge

1 Roll out the flower paste thinly and turn it over before cutting out the flower. This way, you will get a cleaner edge.

2 Either place the flower on a foam pad and shape with a ball tool or press it into a blossom veiner. Set the flower aside on some crumpled foil or ridged piece of sponge.

3 The blossom centres are piped with royal icing. This is easier to do once they have been stuck on to the cupcakes.

folded blossoms

To create folded blossoms, thinly roll out some flower paste and cut out a blossom as opposite (I usually use a five-petal blossom cutter for this). Fold the blossom in half and half again, then pinch at the base, removing any excess paste. Set the blossom aside to dry.

roses

I use two methods for making roses: rolled roses and a cone method. Both have a slightly different look and one is quicker than the other.

cone method

This method is used to make larger, more realistic roses, and although it is more time-consuming, it produces a gorgeous flower. You will need to make the centre cone at least a few hours in advance. Roses can be made in different sizes, but larger cones will need to dry out overnight.

you will need

♡ flower paste

♡ cocktail sticks (toothpicks)

♡ cake dummy

♡ non-stick board with non-slip mat

♡ non-stick rolling pin

♡ rose petal cutters

♡ foam pad

♡ ball tool

♡ edible glue

1 To make the cone centre, roll a small ball of flower paste and squeeze together one side by making a 'V' with the palm of your hands. Push a cocktail stick (toothpick) into the base and set aside to dry in a cake dummy.

2 Roll out the flower paste thinly and cut out six petals per rose. The size of the petal cutter you use should be slightly larger than the height of the cone. Place them on the foam pad and soften the edges with a ball tool. Carefully use a cocktail stick (toothpick) to curl back the tops of three of the petals for the third layer. If you are making lots of roses, only work on a few at a time.

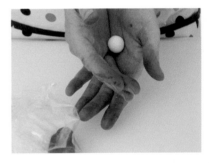

3 Take your cone centre and wrap one of the petals around the cone. Stick it down with some edible glue (see p. 94).

4 The next layer is made up of two petals that you wrap around the centre petal. Tuck the left side of each petal underneath the other one. Use edible glue to secure. Repeat this with the remaining three curled-back petals for the third layer.

5 Cut out 12 more, slightly larger petals from the flower paste and then soften and curl with a cocktail stick (toothpick) as before. Use five of them for the fourth layer and the remaining seven as the outer layer. Tuck each one underneath one side of the next and stick in place with edible glue. Try to keep the spacing even between each petal.

6 Tease the petals out with your fingers to form a lovely shaped rose and set aside to dry.

You can keep your flower paste or cut petals under a plastic bag or mat to prevent the icing from drying out while you work on the other petals

rolled roses

Rolled roses are really quick and easy to make. You can add additional petals if you want to create a larger rose or bud. For a cost-effective alternative, use modelling paste combined with flower paste, especially if you are making your own modelling paste (see p. 95).

you will need

♡ flower paste

♡ cellophane sleeve

♡ white fat (shortening)

1 Roll the paste into a long thin sausage shape about 7mm (¼in) in diameter. Cut 3–4cm (1¼–1½in) pieces and place them into the cellophane sleeve that has been lightly greased with white fat (shortening) to prevent sticking.

2 Press down on one edge to make a flat surface along one side, leaving the other side fairly thick.

3 Take each piece at a time and roll one end inwards to form your rose. Pinch at the base and pull away any excess paste.

4 If you are adding extra petals around the rolled rose, flatten ball shapes on one side between the cellophane and cup them around the rolled rose centre.

making bows

Bows are a lovely decoration and are really easy to make. Those featured in the projects in the book are all different sizes, but are created in the same way. Larger bows may need support with kitchen paper (paper towels) or tissue as they dry so that they hold their shape and don't collapse.

you will need

- ♡ flower paste
- ♡ non-stick board
- ♡ small non-stick rolling pin
- ♡ sharp knife
- ♡ edible glue
- ♡ paintbrush

1 Roll out an oblong piece of flower paste. Cut two long strips of equal widths: one to make the loops and the other to form the two tails. You will also need a small strip of paste of equal width to make the knot.

2 Take one of the strips and pinch the centre. Fold the two ends inwards to the centre and glue in place. Pinch everything together and wrap the small piece of paste between the loops to make the knot.

3 Cut the other long strip in half to make the tails. You can cut the ends at an angle or keep them straight. Stick the two ends that go under the knot of the bow together before sticking on the bow.

4 Allow the bow to dry a little before attaching it to your cupcake. Don't let it dry out completely, as it won't sit naturally on the cupcake. Once the bow is in place, set aside to dry.

using moulds

Silicone moulds are a fantastic invention and are used throughout this book for various decorations. I prefer to use flower paste for these decorations, as they are all very small. But if you are making larger decorations, you could use modelling paste.

To make moulded decorations, press a ball of paste about the same size as the shape you are making into the mould. Grease the mould well with white fat (shortening) or dust with edible lustre dust or cornflour (cornstarch) before inserting the icing into the mould so that it comes out easily. Use a sharp knife or a small palette knife to cut away any excess paste.

dusting with edible lustre

Brushing or painting edible lustre dust on to your decorations makes them glisten beautifully and really stand out.

Individual decorations that require lustre can be dusted with a soft brush before sticking them on to the cupcakes. For decorations already attached in place or small specific details, you will need to paint the lustre on. To do this, add a small amount of clear alcohol to the powder until you have a good consistency to paint with and then apply with a fine paintbrush.

storage

Cupcakes are best eaten the same day as they are made so that they are as fresh as possible. However, this isn't always practical, as you need plenty of time to decorate them, especially if there is quite a lot of detail involved. If the cakes are completely covered in icing, this will help to preserve the moisture in the cake. Any undecorated cooled cupcakes can be stored in an airtight container.

You can freeze the baked cupcakes as soon as they are cool and thaw them when you are ready to decorate them

transport

There is a wide variety of boxes and containers available today made especially for transporting and storing cupcakes. Alternatively, stick cupcakes down on to a large square cake drum covered with royal icing and put them in a normal cake box. Make sure this is done well in advance so that the icing sets hard before you move them.

presentation

How you choose to present your cupcakes will depend very much on the occasion, but here are a few ideas:

cake stands and plates

There are so many beautiful cake stands and plates available now to really show off your lovely little masterpieces. Dot them around on small glass and ceramic stands or pile them up high on one large perspex one.

individual boxes

These are perfect for making a gift of your cupcakes. Stick the cake down with royal icing so that it can't move about in the box. Tie some lovely satin or sheer ribbon around to finish it off.

cupcake wrappers

Cupcake wrappers have recently become very popular and they are available in a range of interesting designs. Choose one to complement the decoration on your cake.

templates

All templates are shown at actual size.

secret admirer (p. 12): mask

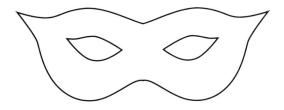

lovebirds (p. 18): birds

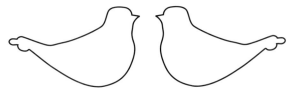

forget-me-not (p. 54): butterfly wing 'run-out'

city of love (p. 22): eiffel tower

suppliers

UK

Zoe Clark Cakes
161 Astonville Street
London
SW18 5AQ
Tel: 020 8874 2519
Email: info@zoeclarkcakes.com
www.zoeclarkcakes.com

Baker's Boutique
Tel: 020 8333 1559
www.thebakersboutique.com

Blue Ribbons
29 Walton Road
East Molesey, Surrey
KT8 0DH
Tel: 020 8941 1591
www.blueribbons.co.uk

CelCakes and CelCrafts
Springfield House
Gate Helmsley, York
YO41 1NF
Tel: 01759 371447
www.celcakes.co.uk

Squire's Kitchen
3 Waverley Lane
Farnham, Surrey
GU9 8BB
Tel: 0845 61 71 810
www.squires-shop.com

US

Global Sugar Art
625 Route 3
Unit Plattsburgh
NY 12901
Tel: 1-518-561-3039
www.globalsugarart.com

Abbreviations used in this book

CK – CelCakes and CelCrafts
DS – Designer Stencils
FI – First Impressions
HH – Hawthorne Hill
PME – PME Sugarcraft
SS – Sunflower Sugarcraft

US cup measurements

If you prefer to use cup measurements, please use the following conversions.
(Note: 1 Australian tbsp = 20ml)

liquid
1 tsp = 5ml
1 tbsp = 15ml
½ cup = 125ml/4fl oz
1 cup = 225ml/8fl oz

butter
1 tbsp = 15g/1/2oz
2 tbsp = 25g//1oz
½ cup/1 stick = 115g/4oz
1 cup/2 sticks = 225g/8oz

caster (superfine) sugar/brown sugar
½ cup = 100g/31/2oz
1 cup = 200g/7oz

icing (confectioners') sugar
1 cup = 115g/4oz

flour
1 cup = 140g/5oz

desiccated (dry unsweetened shredded) coconut
1 cup = 90g/31/4oz

chopped nuts
1 cup = 150g/51/2oz

cream cheese/plain yogurt/ double (heavy) cream
1 cup = 225g/8oz

about the author

Zoe's intricate style of cake design has drawn praise from both clients and press. Her work is regularly featured in national bridal magazines as an inspiration to those getting married and she has made several appearances on wedding shows on TV.

This is Zoe's second book. Her first, *Cake Decorating at Home*, is also published by David & Charles.

acknowledgments

Many thanks to Sian Irvine for the amazing photography, the editor Beth Dymond and everyone at David & Charles for making this book a reality. I'd also like to thank Zita Elze (www.zitaelze.com) and The Crockery Cupboard (www.thecrockerycupboard.co.uk) for supplying the beautiful flowers and props used in the photo shoots.

Last but not least, I'd like to thank my family for all their love, support and enthusiastic cake tasting. Without them, this book would not have been possible.

index